A
POWERFUL WOMAN

Myra Rutledge

To order additional copies of this book, contact:
Xlibris Corporation
1-888-795-4274
www.Xlibris.com
Orders@Xlibris.com
38346

CONTENTS

I'M FLYING HIGH

I'm flying high, but not in a machine.
I'm flying high, no wings on my back.
I'm flying high, my life is on the narrow track.
I'm flying high, I am a real life Queen.
I'm flying high, I don't do the drug scene.
I'm flying high, smiles are all over my face,
I'm flying high, I'm so amazed at how high I'm flying.

To breathe in this human race inspire me to travel the highest heights.
To live not just for the moment, but for all that is right!
I have the seat belts of righteousness tightly buckled about my waist,
It may be a bumpy ride at times, but I won't lose the faith.

I'm flying high, higher than a mountain's peek.
I'm flying high, higher than birds nestling in the trees.
I'm flying high, higher than a mezzo-soprano's high note.
I'm all the way up there with the clouds and rising chimney smoke.

I'm flying so very high!
I have the promises of God embedded safely within my heart!
For these reasons alone,
I   C A N   F L Y!!!!!!!

GOD'S DELIGHT

Imagine life in glory,
forgetting this world and its worries,
dancing from cloud to cloud,
resting on angel wings,
rejuvenating on God's breathe,
then sliding down a rainbow to make
a splash in Heaven's pond.

A spirit forever
praising,
singing,
rejoicing,
just to be "God's Delight" throughout eternity.

LOVE'S SPIRIT

Love will conquer pain,
and render a heart from its strain.

Love will endure the test of time,
and Christians are to love at all times.

Love's strength will put the enemy's plot to shame,
and only love will persevere and rejoice in Jesus name!

YES I CAN

Yes!

I can do it!
Whatever it may be!

No!
I will not be bothered with no I can't!
No is not me!

I can do all things through Christ!
He strengthens my soul,
and only in Him am I strong and bold!

If Jesus dwells within me—Yes!
I can do it!
Yes is me!

ABOUT MY FATHER'S BUSINESS

I am to be about my father's business,
wherever I be and whatever I do.
The world must know that His Spirit lives within me,
so He will be glorified and the world set free.

Temptations abound,
hatred surround,
enemies roam,
trying to keep me from meeting Him who sits on the throne.

I am to be about my father's business,
continually praying and meditating on His Word.

The harvest is plentiful,
and laborers are few,
I can't live life the way sinners do!

I am to be about my father's business,
feeding the hungry,
laying hands on the sick,
clothing the poor,
saving the lost through prayer and testimonies,
spreading the "Good News" from country to country.

I am to be about my father's business,
not a gossip,
not a busy body,
but a vessel pleasing to the Lord,
a woman after God's own heart!

MY CHILDREN

I want my children to be saved by God's grace!
I want them to always hope and grow in faith!
I desire my children to have a true righteous behavior,
and to never be ashamed to confess Christ as their Lord and Savior!

On life's journey, before yielding to temptation,
I pray the Lord give them mercy,
and they seek salvation.

I pray they will remember to always put God first,
then I know they will be satisfied whenever they hunger or thirst!
I pray they will always do their best,
and in working hard they will find true happiness and success!

I know my children are gifts from God,
to love,
to nurture,
and give a healthy start!
While mother's milk gave them strong bones,
Words from the Lord will help them to continue own!

When they are adults with families too,
in guiding their children they will know what to do!
Pass it on throughout the generations,
that God is Love and He is in all creation!

O' PRAISE THE LORD

O' Praise the Lord while there is life in your veins!

Praise Him with great boldness!
Never be ashamed to exalt the Name!

Praise Him!
Lift up His Holy Name!

Praise Him!
Praise the Lord!

Our Savior!
Our God!

GOD IS THE AUTHOR OF TALENT

God is the Author of talent,
He gives to each the amount that is do,
He does not hesitate when it comes to giving,
So why must you?

Be a prosperous vessel, achieve all you can.
God is faithful and freely gives to each man.
Don't be selfish and hold back from others.
When it is in your power to act, help your brother!

Show caring through sharing,
say encouraging words.
Be of good encouragement,
don't allow envy and resentment.

Seek a humble spirit,
do everything in love.
When it comes to talent,
it is gifted from above.

A POWERFUL BLACK WOMAN

I am a powerful black woman,
the wind greets me with a dance,
longevity runs through my veins.
I will speak with my voice,
words of truth and not be ashamed!

Strong and free!
The world is looking at me!
I open my arms and spread love around to those broken and bound.
I am the example of how to fight!
God is my refuse!
God is my might!
I pray and know God will answer!
I am a powerful black woman—saved and free!

Two is better than one,
I have the Father, the Holy Ghost, and the Son!
There is no battle too great for me,
through perseverance—not strife—I stand still and win!
I may be tempted, but not overcome by sin!

I am a powerful black woman!
The world knows I am blessed!
I do God's will, and whatever I ask—He gives!

My children are like olive shoots sprouting around my table,
I have instructed them well—they know God is able!
I walk by faith and not by sight!
God says my family is saved,
I say all is right!

While living this life in time,
demons come to confuse my mind,
but I am a powerful black woman!
My stronghold is Jesus—I rest in HIM!

WHY MUST I STAND AT HELL'S GATE?

I never believed this would be me.
I never realized this would happen to me.
I went to church and sung in the choir,
I went to Bible studies each week,
and was filled with the fire of the spirit.
I paid my tithes and never was late,
SO WHY MUST I STAND AT HELL'S GATE?

I stayed to myself,
I didn't need anybody's help,
I understood why Jesus swept.
There were some I despised for not doing your will,
and I placed myself above the "run of the mill."
I prayed for the poor and dishearten,
so I didn't have to share a dime or my time.
I even prayed for the people I had to hate,
SO WHY MUST I STAND AT HELL'S GATE?

I felt some envy when others succeeded me.
I was careful not to mention your joy to the unsaved
people I would meet,
for your word is convicting,
so I erected a ploy.
I had to think of the feelings I would hurt.
I was always careful not to have a fanatical trait,
SO WHY MUST I STAND AT HELL'S GATE?

Lord, Lord, what went wrong?
Heaven should be my eternal home,
I didn't bother people,
I just left them alone.
I only talked about those who went astray.
Remember those days when I would fast and pray?
Remember those Sundays when I would shout?
I would jump and dance about the place.
The Holy Ghost was all around,
but Lord, Lord, why should I be hell bound?
I knew others in that church were just fakes,
SO WHY MUST I STAND AT HELL'S GATE?

I WOULD DO WHAT MY MAMA SAY

Sipping sugar sweeten ice cold lemonade,
thinking, while drinking,
taking a bite of a banana and peanut butter sandwich on white bread,
being careful not to drip the pickled spread,
yet doubtful, but still contemplating on convincing my Mama to let me go.

Swaying back and forth in the old faded swinger,
feeling a faint breeze from the dogwood trees,
watching the sun bake everything in sight,
as my solemnest rested on the coming night.

Hair up in corn-rolls, pink sandal shoes revealing freshly polished toes,
left hand goes up, waving at nosey old lady across the street,
"Oh yes Mrs. Nix." I say to myself. "I am young and wearing "short-shorts,"
and this is definitely a halter top, My Mama says it is okay,
so you just have yourself a good old woman's day."

The phone rings, it is for me.
My boyfriend says he has his Dad's new car and will pick me up at 7:30.
I turn around to look at my Mama, she is shaking her head,
my emotions erupt like a loud thunder.

Can't go here! Can't go there!
I am 16 years old and can't go nowhere!

"Oh, to bring those youthful days back,
I would have more sense,
I would use more tact."

"I would love to lounge on that front porch again,
and feel the comfort of home back then,
to wave at the neighbors walking up and down the street,
and to seek cautions in the friends I would meet."

The smell of fried chicken was coming from under the kitchen door,
as I shouted to my Mama, "I'm going to the corner store."
She loudly shouted back, "For what are you going up there for?
I never answered, while hurriedly walking away.

My boyfriend was waiting to take me on a spin,
That car was glistening new and shinny,
I just jumped right on in!
We drove up and parked on lovers lane hill,
drinking cheap wine and fornicating until we were fulfilled.
"Oh!" I shouted. "My Mama's gonna kill me!"
Looking at his watch, I saw it was almost 9:30!

While he was pulling up his pants,
I didn't give him a chance,
I started the car up and it was somehow knocked out of gear,
It rolled down the hill, now I am here . . . .

"Oh to bring back that day, I would do what my Mama say."

PAULINE
(A quicken spirit)

As leaves grow continually on a vine,
and aged wine is pleasing to the stomach's core,
so will love for Pauline remain in the heart,
sweetly aging forevermore.

A sister of beauty,
her spirit quickens,
her soul now rest with God.
Her body is still,
but only until that great getting up day,
when we shall all meet Jesus face to face.

WHERE THE FLOCK COMES TO MEET

It is just a building,
brick,
stone,
wood.

It is just a building,
four walls,
a roof.

A very lovely place where the flock comes to meet.
A sturdy building dedicated to God.
Stained class windows,
cathedral ceilings,
cushioned seats,
where the flock comes to meet.
Dressed in silks and satins,
ties for each tailored suit.

Gold trimmed pulpits where preachers come to stand,
while dressed in the eloquent royal robe.
But it is still just a building.
He is only a man.

Oh, but when the anointing is ushered in
through prayer, singing, preaching
and Bible based teaching,
yokes are then broken, souls are saved,
and praising hands makes that devil behave.

It is not in the building.
It is not in the clothes.
It is what's nettled in the heart's vessel
and how it feeds the soul.

HE KNEW

Before I even prayed for a baby girl,
the Lord knew who you were,
He knew your name.

The Lord knew your place in this world
before you were even in my womb,
and before I went through the birthing pain
of delivering you on that warm spring afternoon.

He knew that in your childhood,
you would have a stubborn spirit.
He knew that in your youth,
you would become rebellious while
mixing with your peers at school.
And in your parents chastising,
He knew you would only despise us for a moment,
then everything would be okay,
after we bowed, as a family, to pray.

I knew that carrying a baby would change my body's form and lifestyle.
I already loved you though,
because God was blessing me with a little child to nurture and watch grow.

After nine months of waiting I kissed your tiny face,
I counted little toes and fingers and welcomed you to this human race.
I loved you even before God sent you to me,
and thanked the Lord for carrying us through,
my husband, my child and me.

ONE SOUL SPECIAL TO GOD

To retire means to close one door,
to turn around,
to open one more.
Doors of opportunity reign supreme,
all achievements begin in a dream.

One is here to leave a mark,
One precious person,
One tender heart.
One is here abiding in time,
savoring the moments,
sipping life's wine.

A diamond of a jewel,
A perfumed rose,
A figurine of a person,
God's living soul.

You should continue to prosper,
your work is not done,
through love and laughter you usher in the sun.

Throughout your life you have been blessed,
for God's people there is nothing less.
True friends and family will abide,
Never give up!
Never weaken your stride!

Remember who you are,
One precious person,
One tender heart,
One Soul Special to God.

LOVED A MAN

Loved a man once,
asked him to marry me,
didn't get no response.

He asked me to come live with him.
This being his escape,
didn't want to lose him,
didn't hesitate.

In going through the motions of everyday life,
I prayed,
"God let him take me as his wife."
I cooked,
I cleaned,
catering to his every whim,
I loved him.

Five years later nothing had changed,
I asked him again for his last name.
He looked at me and said, "Baby,
we don't need a piece of paper to stay this course,
why marry when there is a high rate in divorce?

I gave birth to a baby boy,
just what he wanted, his little joy.
The next year a little girl came.
I asked again, "Please give me your name."
"Baby," He said, "You are still my woman,
I love you,
you love me,
the two of us is all we need."

Twenty years passed on by,
Looking down at my ring finger, I was brought to tears.
"Dear Lord make this man marry me,
I have loved him all these years."

Into the menopausal of my life,
I still love this man.
So now, he takes a younger woman to become his legal wife.
And In all those years of praying I never asked the Lord for spiritual advise,
only that he would make me this man's earthly wife.

WICKEDLY SEDUCTIVE NIGHT

Awakening to the faint morning's light,
passion was still strong.
Reaching sleepily for another condom,
he secured it tightly around his excitement.
Her genitals still moist and warm,
solicited another rouse for the road.
This guy was all she needed,
body healthy and strong!

Meeting just hours before at the club,
she wore a tight fitting tube top and low rider jeans
that hugged her wide hips,
to reveal her booty's crack,
whenever she'd take a sudden dip on the dance floor.

He was seated at the bar drinking long Island Tea's,
and watched her shake her booty to the rap's beat,
craving her body's heat.

Eye contact.
They knew the deal.
Nothing else mattered.
Do what you feel.

With no promises of ever meeting again,
they rented a room as a lover's den.

This was not new to either of them.
They only sometimes worried about contacting a disease,
but false belief in condoms assured them of no HIV.

Hours later, she looked at the clock,
then hurried for her clothes.
He rolled over asking, "Where you gotta go?"
She looked back, hands on the exit door, "It is Sunday morning,
I have fed this flesh all night,
gotta go to church, gotta get my soul fed right!
Then ask forgiveness for this wickedly seductive night!"

THE MODERN DAY CHRISTIAN WOMAN

She gets up in her morning, it may be evening,
late night or early with the sun,
depending on the shift she worked the day or night before,
then she prays before beginning her daily runs.

She may be a single parent,
or there might be a husband at home,
she may have children or she might be living alone.
Whichever life she is living,
she is always cheerfully giving,
she asks for a fresh anointing each day,
and never forgets to humbly pray.

If she is a single woman,
God is her husband.
If a gentleman is in her life,
she cautions him,
saying, "I am not yet your wife."

If she is a married woman,
she is yoked with her man,
embracing God's blessing,
and enjoying the Christian living.

In her night, before she goes to bed,
at the bowing of her head,
she is on her knees praying
and asking forgiveness for wrongs done in her day.
If she dies before she awakes,
"Dear Lord," she prays,
"my soul you take."

AN INVITATION TO PRAISE

If you died this moment,
would your soul be at rest?
Are you giving God your very best?
Have you been saved from what is to come?
Why are you so calm in holding back the praise?

When the Choir starts to sing will you be in public shame,
once others around you start lifting Jesus' name?
Don't stare in amazement,
Get up!
Come glorify the Lord with us!
Don't be still, holding resentment, as to cause a fuss!

O' come with us and feel the presence of the Lord this day!
If you feel the fire,
don't harden your hearts and be in dismay!
Bow those heads!
Pray!
Wave those hands!
Stomp loud those feet!
Invite the anointed rhythm inside,
take this Holy Ghost ride!

O' invite the rhythm!
Dance with the blaze of the spirit's fire!
Don't be dignified and sit there in those seats!
Get engulfed with the spirit's heat!

Only when you allow the spirit to take control,
will you understand that the Kingdom of God is within you,
and praise is something you normally should do!

Praise Him! Praise the Lord with instruments and loud voice!
Praise Him! Praise the Lord with a new song and rejoice!

As King David danced so humbly in praise before the Lord,
wearing only a linen ephod,
Give the Lord love from the soul and the heart,
come worship in praise this day!

HE WILL

When nobody else believes in me,
I will believe in myself.
When nobody else wants me to succeed,
my faith is strong—I still shall believe!

I have prayed that the Lord will open a door,
and he will—just for me!

You may not understand my dreams,
they may not seem real to you.

You may tell me I'm reaching too high,
that only clouds dance in the sky.

I'm free in the Lord,
His Word has taken root in my heart.

My faith is strong!

No doubting here!

I have no fear!

I shall move on!

I have prayed that the Lord will open a door,
and he will—just for me!

BELIEVE, SEEK, RECEIVE

You must **believe** in your heart,
confess with your mouth,
that Jesus Christ is Lord.

You must **seek** the gift of the Holy Ghost,
the anointing that frees the soul.

Jeremiah said, "Its like fire shut up in the bones."

Our comforter,

our friend,

our deposit to God's Heavenly home.

You must **receive** the gift of the Holy Ghost,
the anointing that frees the soul.

TRUST IN THE LORD

Show love in everything you do,
trust in the Lord,
He will see you through!

When trouble comes,
cry out to God!
Faith will rescue that aching heart,
trust in the Lord!

Don't ever be afraid,
trust in the Lord!

Discard all cares,
fears and doubts,
trust in the Lord,
He will help you out!

IT'S ALL IN JESUS

It's all in Jesus,
It's all in Him.
It's all in Jesus,
It's all in Him.

From the beginning,
throughout life's end.
It's all in Jesus,
It's all in Him.

When the Lord made this earth,
all was well that lived and dwelled.
There was no time.
There was no curse.

He made the man over all creation,
no boundaries set, no limitations.
He made us to trust and obey,
but man's evil heart went astray.

No need to worry,
No need to fret,
God's love for us sent Jesus
to pay our sin debt.
So seek and you shall find.
Seek the Lord while there is still time.

NEVER ALONE

From the beginning of time,
there has been countless sickness and devastating crime,
multiple heartaches and disappointments.

For these reasons our Jesus was sent,
a name above all others ever known,
He is here and we are never alone.

This World keeps changing day to day.
Its getting harder to walk the Christian way,
but God will never leave us to face this World
without his love, mercy and grace.

Whenever the devil comes to steal away your joy,
remember Jesus died at Calvary to thwart that ploy.

Call on him!
Call on him!
You are never alone!

PLEASE RELEASE ME

I did not know,
I did not seek to find.

The Preacher always said
Jesus was a friend of mind,
but now I am here to face my destiny.
Please release me.

I did not go to church with my family,
I stayed at home, slept or watched TV,
but now I am here in eternity,
Please release me.

I lived life not redeeming the time,
I did whatever came to this carnal mind,
I never reverence Jesus Christ as Lord,
and I did not place His Word in this foolish heart.

I did not know,
I did not seek to find,
the Preacher always said,
Jesus was a friend of mind,
but now I am here in my destiny,
Please release me.

WELL DONE

I don't care what they say,
I'm going to do things the Lord's way.
I don't care what they think about me,
I'm looking upwards toward the Heavenlies.

I'm going to follow my heart.
They can laugh,
throw a foot or two in my path,
but they can't make me fall.
I am forever standing tall.
Someday I'm going to hear Jesus say,
Well done my good and faithful servant—well done!

JESUS IS A FRIEND

In the arms of God we can find our way,
Whenever we are sad and lonely.
He has given us liberty,
It is all in Jesus only.
He is the Savior for all mankind,
No greater love will we ever find.

Jesus is a Friend,
He once came as God in the Flesh,
to redeem a dying world from this sinful mess.

Sitting at the right side of God,
Jesus is ever interceding,
He is there waiting,
just ask him into your heart,
He's the only Savior and God.

A TALE OF ONE RICH MAN

Once a man thought being rich was all there was,
he worked, invested, put money above love.
Within the sweat, hard work and saving,
he amassed a fortune other men were craving.

There was nothing he could not buy,
his limit on material possessions was the sky.
Parties, caviar, champagne and extravagant women,
his indulgence of them all were quite plenty.

He had so much pride.
So boldly he would boast,
"I have more money than most."
A self made man known throughout the land,
because of his wealth he was loved.

One day he took an inventory of all that was his,
he became sadden while thinking and
said, "I have so much but
no family, I need to get busy, I need a wife and kids."

His riches bought security in life,
he could pay any woman to be his lover or wife,
he could buy a home anywhere he please,
he could sail his yacht across all the seas,
he could fly his private jet to any city,
but in his life he felt empty.

He decided to make a change,
slow the pace a bit,
help a few charities,
maybe this would rid the emptiness that had come over him.
There is power in money, that fact is well known,
so he offered to help a few people find better homes.

Mr. Charity himself, he became,
lavishing in the new found fame.
On TV and radio he would go.
He wanted the entire world to know.
It was so great, for goodness sake, let him tell how
he gave the most tax deductible donations
to homeless people hit by an earthquake.

Eventually the charity work became tiresome,
In his heart, for a family he was still lonesome.
After they signed a contractual agreement,
both had mutually consented to this marriage of convenience.
He wanted to produce an heir of his own,
her mind had already "planned" a palace style home.

He found that his wife could not conceive,
so they adopted a baby,
it was found to be lazy,
so they put it away in the appropriate home,
and there it stays without love—all alone.

The new investments paid big,
thanks to the internet companies and all they did.
More richer than before,
wife number one walks out the door.
Poor rich man,
feeling empty again,
still not realizing his "short-comings."

Partying, wild women, and drinking,
maybe a little drugs to distort his thinking.
Another woman he takes as a bride,
she is along just for the ride.
A pretty young flower,
out for what she can get,
If the romance gets sour,
she has had a couple of kids for permanent benefits.

On his 50th birthday he takes another inventory,
and comes to this reveling story,
"I have done all to get to where I am,"
He starts to boast.
"I certainly have the most. These riches will protect me from the struggles of life,
I have two kids and a beautiful young wife.
I am a self made man, look at all I have done while living in this life."

MY LOVE

I desire for you to touch my face and kiss these lips,
rubbing those large hands across these voluptuous hips,
I know the feeling is mutual,
we are at passion's door.

Oh come and kiss these quivering lips again,
bring yourself to me and wrap me in the blanket of your sweet loving.
We lay together 'til the morning's dew glistens at the window's pane,
and the sweet sounds of little birdies singing gleeful in the trees
are heard at our awakening.

I have saved myself for you my love,
you have saved yourself for me.
I know our relationship may seem unusual,
but this is how God intended for marriage to be.

THIS AND THAT

I am the head and not the tail,
my Lord tells me this.

I can have my soul's desire,
my Lord tells me that.

I should be a lender,
not a borrower,
my Lord tells me this.

I should love the Lord with all my
soul and all my heart,
my Lord tells me that.

I should give freely as he has done,
my Lord tells me this.

I should find comfort in his Word,
my Lord tells me that.

I should ask and receive,
my Lord tells me this.

I should always be thankful and believe,
my Lord tells me that.

So, I should never forget,
this and that.

O' THANK YOU JESUS

O' Thank You Jesus for letting
me see another day.
O' Thank You Jesus for leading
me on the narrow way.

People can say what they want about me,
it won't benefit in the least,
because I've got a mind to praise the Lord,
I Love to serve the Lord.

He brought me out of darkness
into a blessed land.

I thank you Jesus,
forever raising up my hands
to Praise the Lord,
to Serve the Lord!

JESUS IS THE ROCK

We were lost and discarded,
bruised for disobeying,
our righteous stand with God
was quickly, quickly fading.

To be reconciled again,
he sent grace and mercy for sin.
Praise to God for giving us Jesus!

Jesus is the rock of our salvation,
through only him is all creation,
through only him are we redeemed.
Praise to God for giving us Jesus!

GOD'S WORD REMAINS THE SAME

God says for mankind not to steal,
he made this plain to us more than 2000 years ago.
He means not to take what is not yours,
but masked men are always out robbing clothing, banks and grocery stores.

God made it plain that we are not to kill,
but anger promotes death everyday.
It might have been something that was said,
or a look that was given in a certain way.
A gun is fired or a knife is drawn,
then another lost soul exits before another day dawns.

God told us not to have any other gods before him,
but our jobs, our clothes, jewelry, money and other things,
we allow to dominate our very being.

We are not to use his name in vain,
but some carelessly call on Jesus
and profane his name and God's,
not honoring Jesus as Lord.

A Sabbath day should be Holy to the Lord,
but what do we do but harden our hearts.
We turn our heads away from what God has proclaimed and
believe that within two thousand years his Word must have changed.

God says to honor our Father and our Mother,
but so many parents don't know this scripture or even how to pray,
don't even know or care that this is what the Bible says.
Raising rebellious children with no respect for the aged,
possessing a stiff neck and deaf ear whenever their
children are disruptive and misbehave.
So how can a child honor a parent when they were selfishly raised?

God says for us not to commit adultery.
Get your own husband!
Get your own wife—marry!
Make a vow to the Lord that you will love each other
with your whole hearts,
forsaking all others,
gleaning to each other.
But there is so much distraction
going on these days,
more women are loose with their bodies,
men are too.

God says for us not to lie about our neighbors.
We should attend to our own business,
abhor the spirit of misguided behavior.

God says for us not to covet what others have.
Don't allow the spirit of Jealousy and envy to sprout,
love each other for prospering.
Yours is coming too—just never doubt!

You should love the Lord your God with all your heart and soul.
It has been over 2000 years,
and this is still how it is.
God's word never will change,
his Words for our lives remain the same.

I DESIRE TO BE REAL

What am I to do Lord?
I'm so ashamed.
I try to do right,
but wrong still remain.
I try to be faithful by doing your will,
but sometime I just can't be still.

I'm not what I should be.
I don't pray continually.
I should increase my works,
and not forsake the services at church.
I should always be diligent to your word.

I confessed Christ at an early age,
now I know there is much more in being saved.
My desire is to be real,
inside and out.
My desire is to be delivered from anguish and doubts.

Lord, renew my heart.
Lord, renew my soul.
My dear Jesus take full control!

Give me a loving spirit.
Give me gentle hands comforting to the soul,
and a heart that understands.

I know you are there whenever I'm in despair,
I know you are faithful and always care.

My desire is to be real,
inside and out.
My desire is to be delivered from anguish and doubts.

STAND STILL

The enemy comes to steal,
kill,
destroy.

Liken to a lion waiting to devour its prey.
O' don't worry,
stand still,
pray.

Let God fight the battle,
Holy and in the Christian way.

O' don't worry,
stand still,
proclaim.
Get thee behind me Satan in Jesus name!

Demons tremble at the name Jesus,
the only name given under Heaven to free us.
Use God's Word as the weapon of choice,
dividing like a two-edged sword,
causing the enemy to hasten and all God's people freely rejoice.

Stand still,
speak.
Mountains must move.
Stand still in faith,
you won't ever lose.

We must use God's Word as the weapon of choice,
dividing like a two-edged sword,
causing the enemy to hasten and all God's people freely rejoice.

HAVE FAITH

Faith is the key to whatever your dreams may be,
only believe, then you shall receive.

Never neglect to pray to shatter delays,
strong will and determination overcome all limitations.

Have faith, there is no other way,
never forget to pray,
trust and obey.

Mountains are high but are made low,
once prayer is heard all obstacles must go.

Trouble comes only to make us strong,
don't dwell on the problem,
you have got to move on.

Faith is the key for you and me,
only believe, then you are set free.
Have faith, there is no other way,
never forget to pray,
trust and obey.

THE REDEEMED

When I see my Father in Heaven,
I will kneel down at his feet.
We will talk about how good he has been to me.
Worldly circumstances will be no more,
only the promises of God will be seated at Heaven's door.

The coolness of his breath will be with me constantly,
the radiance of his presence will be felt throughout eternity.

I will understand the mysteries,
never ceasing to praise!
I will be an angel of his glory,
remembering his saving grace.

For no ear has heard,
No eye has yet seen,
all the Father has in store for all his people,
the blessed redeemed!

A TALE OF A PROSPEROUS SOUL

Pinkee Tooson was born to a slave,
but she lived free all her earthly days.
She cooked and sewed to make a living,
never sacrificing her warmth in giving and
thinking of others before herself.

Happy to welcome strangers passing through on the roads,
they would sit and eat in her humble abode.
She was always joyful to have folks around,
just visiting her made you put your burdens down.

Presented with the uttermost respect in the courtyards,
never once did she gripe that living was hard,
even when her husband drank moonshine whiskey at times,
chased fast women and came home lying.
She only would lift her hands to the sky,
moan her troubles and pray.
Then in her praising time with God,
she joyfully thanked him for answering her broken heart.

She had thirteen children,
all of various hues,
cause her husband was dark as the night,
and her completion was very light.
She raised them all with the "Good News"
that serving the Lord was the right thing to do.

Although her husband's presence was in the home,
Pinkee brought up those children in the fear of the Lord
on her own.

Her faith in the Lord was so strong,
until her husband stopped drinking, lying,
chasing women and attended to his family at home.
Her children excelled in all their endeavors,
and prosperity was hers forever.
Even now, and she is a long time living in glory,
her family's line continues in blessings because of her faith walk story.

YOU THINKING

You thinking you don't need the help of the Lord,
Keep living life as you do.

You thinking you can cuss and fuss,
drinking alcohol all night through.

You thinking you can keep on having sex
with whomever you please,
just as long as you wear protection
to stop the spread of decease.

You thinking you will go to Heaven someday,
well Satan has deceived your mind.

What you gonna do when your life is spent,
and the Devil gets you before you have a chance to repent?

You have to be born again and delivered from carnal sins.
I am told that Heaven is paved with streets of gold and sinners are not
welcomed in.

You thinking!

Stop thinking!

Start seeking the truth!

ANOINT ME

In and out of this temple Lord,
Keep your fire burning in this simple heart.
Anoint me Holy Spirit each day,
fall all over me as I pray.

I need you each moment that is measured.
I need you,
I am your created pleasure.
I am your servant,
You are my Master,
Grant me Lord,
eternal life ever after.

LOVE WILL ALWAYS BE LOVE

Love is a creation of God,
the joining of two hearts.
A man,
A woman,
married to each other,
Godly loving each other.

Love is patience,
understanding,
joy,
a binding of every man,
woman,
girl,
boy.

Love is giving,
living in peace.
In the sanctity of God love will always be love.

Pure,
sweet,
love should stay.
But only if we pray and walk the narrow way.
For in the sanctity of God love will always be love.

I SING HALLELUJAH

You are the morning sun,
the fresh dew drops on a lawn,
the flowers in a meadow,
rain drops on a window.

I sing Hallelujah, the highest praise to you!
I sing Hallelujah, I give it all to you!

You are the very air I breathe,
my future,
my past,
leaves on trees,
the reason birds sing in sweet harmony.

I sing Hallelujah, the highest praise to you!
I sing Hallelujah, I give it all to you!

BE STRONG HOLD ON

Be strong!

Hold on!

Wait—On the Lord!

He will bring all hope into fruition.

Have faith!

Have trust!

Run and don't be weary,
Walk and don't faint,
All strength comes from God!

In His Word He says,
"Don't worry, for I am with you!"
We must continue to pray and fast.
Only what is done for God will last.

Be strong!

Hold on!

Wait—On the Lord!

ARE YOU THAT SOMEBODY?

Are you anxious for the things of this world?
Craving for the diamonds,
lusting after the pearls.

Money enough you never can have,
working three jobs to keep up with your
conceited pals.

Deceitful thinking,
lying,
contemplating theft,
guilty of fornicating,
in love with yourself,
cheating,
talking about others in every meeting.

Are you that somebody talking about Heaven these days?
Are you that same somebody holding to these evil ways?

I NEED, YOU NEED, WE ALL NEED JESUS

He woke us this morning to greet another day.
Let us not forget to pray as we travel life's way.
At times the roads are rocky,
filled with thorns and tears,
we must learn to Praise Him
throughout the hard wears.

I need Jesus.
You need Jesus.
We all need Jesus.
And that's the truth!

Don't hesitate!
Don't debate!
Don't take the time to procrastinate!

I need Jesus.
You need Jesus.
We all need Jesus
And that's the truth!

MY MOTHER'S LOVE

Throughout the years
and all of life's fears,
my mother's love has been so endearing.

My mother has never been one to judge me,
Never has she complained or called me anything
but a child of God.

My mother's love brought me through
in the times when my world was still brand new.
In my childhood,
resting safe in her arms,
near her heart,
she would rock me to sleep
whenever I felt lost and alarmed or couldn't handle defeat.

Now in adulthood her tenderness has prevailed,
and inside of her encouragement my dreams still dwell.
While I was yet unsaved she stood in the gap for me,
Her early prayers were answered and Jesus has set me free!

My mother is meek and humble in spirit,
the mother all should have.
When I sit down and ponder the years,
my mother's love is still so endearing!

MOTHER

Turn each page and then you will see
how time has passed on into history.
Each moment is captured so graceful in time,
but keeps getting better as our lives intertwine.

So now dear Mother these pages are for you,
our lives in picture pages,
stuck together with glue.

You were once a young wife,
feeling hurt and torn,
conception was hard,
then the first baby girl was born.
God saw fit to bless you over again,
with three more girls and two boys
who are now women and men.

Over the years you have been
more than a mother,
and in forsaking all others
you have always been there for us.

Through the laughter and the pain,
through each heartache, at other times, shame.
You have been more than a mother,
more than a friend in helping us start life over again.

SUMMARY

This poetic piece is a collection of Christian Poetry about living. The poet speaks on everything from sex to love between a woman and man, love for God, love for mother and children, and the hypocrisy that some exemplify as Christians.

These poetic words are written to inspire as they make you laugh, think and rejoice in trying to walk a productive Christian journey.

The title of the book, *"A Powerful Woman,"* is named from the poem listed in the book. It is a testament that real power is found in the stronghold of Jesus.

AUTHOR PAGE

Myra Rutledge lives with her husband in Birmingham Alabama. This is her first published work of poetry. She is currently working on a novel and would like to produce a Christian play for nationwide travel.

Her inspiration comes directly from the word of God as she studies the scriptures and understands how the Bible is applied to everyday living.

She wants her gift of writing to be a blessing to others as they struggle with trying to get it right—the Christian Walk. In being a Christian herself, she knows that the walk is never easy but an everyday challenge.